SOJOURNER

To 20
with love,

Gillian

Gillian **Allnutt** was born in 1949 in London but spent half of her childhood in Newcastle upon Tyne. In 1988 she returned to live in the North East. Before that, she read Philosophy and English at Cambridge and then spent the next 17 years living mostly in London, working mostly as a part-time teacher in further and adult education but also as a performer, publisher, journalist and freelance editor. From 1983 to 1988 she was Poetry Editor at *City Limits* magazine.

She has published six collections of poetry: *Spitting the Pips Out* (Sheba, 1981) and *Beginning the Avocado* (Virago, 1987), and from Bloodaxe Books, *Blackthorn* (1994), *Nantucket and the Angel* (1997) *Lintel* (2001) and *Sojourner* (2004). Both *Nantucket and the Angel* and *Lintel* were shortlisted for the T.S. Eliot Prize, and *Lintel* was a Poetry Book Society Choice.

Gillian Allnutt co-edited *The New British Poetry* (Paladin, 1988) and is the author of *Berthing: A Poetry Workbook* (National Extension College/Virago, 1991). She currently teaches creative writing in adult education and works as a writer in schools. From 2001 to 2002 she held a Royal Literary Fund Fellowship at Newcastle and Leeds Universities and from 2002 to 2003 at Newcastle University.

GILLIAN ALLNUTT

Sojourner

BLOODAXE BOOKS

ISBN: 1 85224 669 3

First published 2004 by
Bloodaxe Books Ltd,
Highgreen,
Tarset,
Northumberland NE48 1RP.

www.bloodaxebooks.com
For further information about Bloodaxe titles
please visit our website or write to
the above address for a catalogue.

Bloodaxe Books Ltd acknowledges
the financial assistance of
Arts Council England, North East.

Cover printing by J. Thomson Colour Printers Ltd, Glasgow.

Printed in Great Britain by
Cromwell Press Ltd, Trowbridge, Wiltshire.

For we are strangers before thee, and sojourners,
as were all our fathers: our days on the earth are
as a shadow, and there is none abiding.

I CHRONICLES 29.15

For Katie, my mother

ACKNOWLEDGEMENTS

Acknowledgements are due to the editors of the following publications in which some of these poems first appeared: *Equinox*, *Poetry* ('Convent Girl', 'The New Broom', 'Dolores' Afternoon'), *Poetry London* and *The Rialto*.

'Sojourner' was commissioned by BBC Radio 3 for a pre-concert poetry reading at the Serpentine Gallery, London, which was broadcast on Radio 3 as an interval feature during the BBC Proms 2001.

I am very grateful to The Royal Literary Fund for a Writing Fellowship based at Newcastle and Leeds Universities in 2001-02 and at Newcastle University in 2002-03.

CONTENTS

I

To a Last

There's a lilt to the way you lie.

How is it to be old and looked at woodenly?

Waylaid, is it?

You'd better stay here, by the fire, like my grandmother.

In her flat shoe and her built-up shoe she wouldn't go even as far

as the river. You could have kept her company.

We'd have brought cobnuts which, this year, are everywhere.

Earlier Incarnation, China

(for Nansi Morgan)

Your legs ache now and then
remembering water, the rice plantation
where you walked, up and down, up and down.
Was it with oxen?

                                    Was your face thin
already, a dawn moon? Did you already resemble
the Bodhisattvas of stone I saw in a London museum,
the Buddhas of Compassion?

Catherine in Paris, 1910

My spine is my own in this light, empty room.
My father, Northumbrian.
My collarbone, broken – a stone.
The sea fled with me from home.

how the bicycle shone

and how it shone, she told us, like a little constellation seldom seen
and how the constellation stopped above the sugar-cane
and how, among the sugar-cane, they found the dark-skinned man
and how the man had been stove-in
and how stove-in was still the word her father used about the
        Barbary Allen
and how they left the *Barbary Allen*, by the water, by her lone
and how she was herself, much later, by her lone in London
and how London might as well have been the moon
and how the moon was white, like bone

Bethan

The cairn broke my head.
I knew the sea dearer to me than bird, breath.
I was a borrowing, Mother said.
Like Hilda, born and bred.
The stones of the cairn were strewn about the earth by God.
Hilda mended me like a cracked bird-bath.

The Harmonium

It had handpainted scenes from the life of Habakkuk under the lid,
    she said.
It was hauled from Merthyr Tydfil, to be hid.
Ivor Gurney was going to write for it, a half-Welsh hymn, but he
    never did.
Something like Hymn One Hundred.
He'd made a start, Da said.
Many times she had it mended.
Heart, she said, full of hope and humdrum under the lid.

Hester

Holly hardened, like her.

Her with her knees gnarled.

Who'd shadows of iron, honey, gold
in a drawer.

Who'd pans to scour.

Death held on through January for her.

For the hens in the yard.

She held too, like laughter
hoarded.

The Widow's Mite: Effie, Dumfries, August 1916

Bring out the boots that will no longer need to be repaired.

Bring them to the bare hillside.

Lovely is the harebell.
Still, frail.

I will take up my anger like a torn floorboard,
a bed.

'Thy will be done.' I said.

Dust of the August afternoon is everywhere.

Dust motes.

I'll gather all the holes together here.

A Shepherd's Life:
Paintings of Jenny Armstrong by Victoria Crowe
(for Jane)

Snowbound Cottages

We came to the border.
We came at night to Kittleyknowe.
We crossed her fields of snow
unshepherded. We did not know they were hers.
She did not come to her door.
In our house now we have lit two fires.
We'll be up for hours.

Large Tree Group

What wills her walking under these large trees,
the wire fence with her
and the world by snow accounted for?

Hat, coat, boots, heart
all right

now and long ago the small plantation where she sat
to work it through.

NOTE: The exhibition *A Shepherd's Life* was shown at the Hatton Gallery, Newcastle, in the spring of 2002. A series of paintings made over 20 years by Victoria Crowe depicts the life of her neighbour, Jenny Armstrong, who worked as a shepherd in the Pentland Hills and died in 1985 aged 82. The poems take their titles from the paintings from which they began.

range and semmit

mantelpiece, her best, beyond her
ornament, amendment, more
the old range comprehended by her
her vest, or semmit, aired over the oven door
wood dried over the fire
october, november
behind the two clocks, letters

Winter Interior

Sheep in smirr.

Without shadow now, the snow,
the straw strewn by her.

She reads indoors.

Words grow smaller.

The kettle on the stool waits with her
through winter.

Celebration for Margaret, the Fraser Boy and All the Rest

On the mantelshelf, a rocking-chair.
A soldier with red lips, a trumpeter.
A picture, her father perhaps, a shepherd before her.
Farm of Fairliehope, near Carlops.
Carnations and poppies in a jar.
Poppies like sunk ships.
A spaniel, its front paws on an opened letter.

Jenny at Home

What shall we do with the days wherein we have dwelt,
                                                          my bonie Dearie?

Days of your father, anywhere out on the moor.

Days of salt and straw.

Days of the stalwart woman you were yourself among yowe and
    wether.

What shall we do with the days, halt now but?

Hither and yon.

                                                Ca' them home,
my bonie Dearie, that have been well borne.

Airspun Powder and Bailer Twine

Air explores earth, its everyday alterations.
But the horse, alone on its stand.
The long-handled jar is alone, after its long association with her.
The japanned box of airspun powder.
The white plastic flowers.
Snow disappears.
But the bailer twine, kept, in a loose, useful ravel.

NOTE: The phrase 'my bonie Dearie' is from Robert Burns's song
'Ca' the yowes to the knowes'.

II

In Miss Macauley's Class
(for John Hudson)

we wear the great war of the world about our shoulders
      with impunity. Our words
            are borrowed

from the campaign dead:
      O bloody, bloody, bloody.
            Who's pinched my bloody kettle? 's what we said.

We're part of the hoard of what happened
      at Gallipoli.
            Gallipoli.

Wherever the avid crowd of the dead has drifted
      with its light war-gear
            of laughter,

there we are.
      Wherever.
            Stars, like salt, thrown over the shoulder.

Poppa

He liked to lay down a tune as if it were the truth.
'Morning has broken, like the first morning.'
Nothing broke him, Brodie Anderson Clinging,
not his son's death.

Euphemia in 1949

(for my mother)

She rocks the child reluctantly,
the cradle-muslin rough and thick with war
and, at the window, blackout.
London without light, almost;
bleak, her thoughts.

                        Now through the smirr
her heart breaks, hearing her father
Brodie with his kilt-bright chords,
his 'Clouden side'.

NOTE: 'Clouden side' is mentioned in Robert Burns's song
'Ca' the yowes to the knowes'.

'The Old Town Hall and St Hilda's Church, Middlesbrough' by L.S. Lowry

I am, like the sky, alone.
St Hilda's poor spire pierces me.
As a pen, paper.
Church-wardens like to turn the word *infinity* upon the tongue.
Take their hats off to me.
The old town hall has settled, now, among its files.
Buff-coloured, faded, from the beginning full.
Mislaid.
A letter from the Board among Christmas cards.
Dear Sir, we write to advise you.
1959 already. Middlesbrough.
People forget me.
Like a street-lamp in summer.
Or they were born yesterday and do not know that during the war.

Literature in Childhood

What was literature?

It was, like a dustsheet, shelter.

It was instead of a father. *Wait till your father gets home.*

Instead of a mother, washing alone.

Even instead of a grandmother.

In it there was no war we'd have to keep on trying to get over.

No corridors in literature, no nuns.

All the time, outside literature, fear was going on.

There were sandwiches, Marmite usually, Spam.

The Fifties

There were windows the war had left alone.
Imagine.
A world that would open.

III

Still

On the radio we're talking integration.
In the amicable studio, Christian, Jew, Muslim.
We are the children of Abraham.
The garden is full of arrival, apple blossom, bluebell.
The sheep are restored to their hill.
Even the road, momentarily, still.
Here we are then. Here we dwell.
Home. Dry.
See where the heron comes, taking its time.
It is Sunday morning.
Its legs stick out, stiffly, tidily.
Like someone learning to swim.

Esh Winning, May 2002

Currach

One there was who stretched the hide of heifer over my bare
      willow-bone.
One who, later, put my patches on.
One who loved his own long leather running-stitches.

Black Madonna

Her body is hollowed out like a boat.

She'll have carried Columba from Glencolumbkille to Iona

over the rough and the clear water

with the one oar.

Later he will bear the boat on his rough-hewn back

as if lifting her with her poor cold feet

over the tracks and stiles of Iona.

Lindisfarne

(for Michael McCarthy)

Let's not talk about
leaving the heart
to be looked at
like a script.

Let's talk about
the beehive of the heart,
the cuddy duck of the heart,
the heart's cuthbert.

cuddy duck: a local name for the puffin, Cuthbert's favourite bird.

34

Lay Brother, 12th Century

Among the whelks, that's where we were.
What would we have done without salt water?

When prayer was of no avail
we had a barrowful

of bowls to take it back
in. We were quick

at washing the wounds
in the Abbot's hands.

We had a whale
too, waiting to sail

with the autumn tide. It lay offshore
like God the Father.

Dottle, Donkey-man

Neither nephew nor niece.
During the war, lowered the ride-price to a ha'penny.
Ignored the world beyond the wire, as if sea only.
On the mantelpiece, a small clay one, given him
Glued together.
Lived, as if among deaf men, alone.
Dumb, like one walking into Jerusalem.

At the Friary in Alnmouth

(for Marian Goodwin)

We are looking at Coquet Island in the long blue evening light.
How awkward we are at Compline.
We have no habits.
The smell of the sea is in our hair yet, after supper.
Our hearts are stranded here, transparent, lit
Like jellyfish in the afternoon.
How awkward it is to be at Compline in the long blue evening light
With my old shoulder-bag lying there yet, at my feet.

NOTE: The window behind the altar in the chapel at the Franciscan friary
in Alnmouth is of plain glass and looks out over the sea.

The Fitting at the Friary

For hours, all afternoon, the sea is alone.

Who can help it?

He kneels at the hem of his brother's habit,
his heart.

Earth navigates. It makes its way among stars and nothing.

Could it ever not come home?

Earth's held.

The sea at the sewing-room door unfolds.

IV

Puppet

There are many like me.

I was made in a world of wood and old wives' tales.

I was made, with rings in my head and heels, to hold only
the strings that held me.

Vaclav made me with his several knives.

His middle daughter made me with her milk and silver needle.

I lost my sword at sea when the captain ran off with me
in the play

and Sundays by the Vltava.

I was laid aside, like Czechoslovakia.

My strings were made of raw silk, red, and rotted
at sea and knotted themselves around me.

Old Bredow

(after the drawing by Paula Modersohn-Becker)

Speech is a garland: it doesn't grow.
He made me understand. The tilth
the heart's at home in is a burial ground
for strangers, still, a potter's field.
He kept his coat, its shapeliness and filth, about him,
all he had earned. He kept
his heart of spelt.

From the Artist's Notebook:
After some paintings of girls and women
by Paula Modersohn-Becker

Clara

She must have made up her mind about everything
before she was seven.
Her linen sleeves were clean.
She would have crossed the fields at dawn,
her father's fields, half-sown,
hearing her mother's admonition –
'Take nothing from the woman. Come straight home.'

Agatha

Life couldn't care less about her, I thought,
with her tidied hair.
Later, she'd lapse.
In her plain blue pinafore and unaware
of what I thought,
she'd traipse home through the water-meadows
with their small blue half-hidden flowers.

Eva

I don't know what she knew about it then.
She was alone in her heart, I thought,
more than half-alone.
She asked if I thought she was pretty.
I thought she was like a pale yellow flower.
I wanted a piano for her
and a father.

La Polonaise

Pale.
Parisian, probably.
Poltroon, they said, but then
they wouldn't walk out of their way to look at anyone.
Memory, gone out of her, of mother, God, man.
World without end, wouldn't spin
her.
        She could pose, with a poppy, earn.

Margarethe

What she meant was scoured stone
the churn stood on.
'Be earlier than bone or birdsong
if you'd idle like the sun
at noon,' she said.
She gave the lad not coin but caudle for his load
of advent wood.

Bette

And though she may have been the least Elisabeth
on earth, she bore a son, her John,
who would have loosed the latchet
of her shoe for love
alone.

      The way goes hard with her, of hearing hard,
who hoards his wild, too well remembered words
like marriage lines.

Ursula

'*Gemälde, Gemälde.*' She admires, ignores, the portrait.
Looks me over now, as if I were her daughter,
in the long dim mirror. Is a worrier,
a wind among the ragwort.

                           Is not yet
even loneliness in me, the child, and look, she's brought
a bowl of something hot, tart, from the near wild
other world. 'To warm the little one. *Gut, gut.*'

Gemälde: painting; *gut:* good.

NOTE: Paula Modersohn-Becker lived and worked in the north German artists'
colony of Worpswede. She died, at the age of 31, after giving birth to her first
child in November 1907. The poems were written as if the artist were reflecting
on the lives and characters of her sitters. Each takes a particular portrait as its
subject:

Clara: *Seated Girl*, 1899
Agatha: *Seated Girl*, 1898/9
Eva: *Young Girl with Yellow Flowers in Vase*, 1902
La Polonaise: *Woman with a Poppy*, 1900
Margarethe: *Old Woman with Handkerchief*, 1906
Bette: *Seated Peasant Woman*, 1899
Ursula: *Old Peasant*, 1903

Tilsit, 1918

I remember the mouth of the river, my grandmother,
webbed and unwebbed winters that went with me
by the Baltic.
                    Once there was armistice,
an amber morning. She and I swept quietly.
There were soldiers. What could we brew for them?
Barley and water, bitter small beer.

Tilsit: renamed Sovetsk, in Lithuania.

German Woman, 1945

The war ran into me, like all women.
It made me a light tin spoon.
I was stranded among them,
Soldaten, Soldaten.
I wore a shawl of cloud-coloured wool.
I lived hard by.
How little their marching mattered to me.
Their laughter bruised my bones.

Soldaten: soldiers.

Poland in My Grandmother's Mind

In my grandmother's mind the winter in Poland's interminable.
Water lies in the road by the last potato field, the sky
so low you must stoop to avoid it like a lintel,

stoop, as you ride with the half-thawed load, your father's
war-dishevelled brother with you always
now, between shafts, to the house

that will lift itself, like history, out of the lost and level plain,
though the shtetl's gone.

Anna K., London, 2001

birds in snow

but that birds may be brought, without the brackishness
of the sea, to the too still snow
troubles me

The Belsen Man

(for my father)

He must have looked
    with his long loose shadow
like Christ on the cross
like the rag and bone man with his horse.

NOTE: My father's army regiment helped liberate Belsen.

The Little Cello

Gdynia, 1949

The boat had faded and had no name.
It came with the evening tide.
It was awkward.
The sea brought it in.
It had one oar and half an oar.
The long and the short of it is, the man said aloud.
He was lame.
He had loose dusty trousers, like flour.
Her mother complained about the war,
about the flour.
The boat came over the turquoise water.
It came to Gdynia.
The sun slanted over the side.
The man rowed.
The man rested aloud.
She was about to be seven, she said, in September.
There was no bread to be had, no bread,
no parcel of bread from Poznan.
She'd something in her pocket, she said.
Something she'd.
Something she shouldn't have.
Look, she said. *It could be a soul, a soul made*
of wood.
It lay in her hand without a sound.
She'd found it under her father's pillow, she said,
in his kept bed.
Without strings or pegs, her mother said,
it wasn't any good.
He could exchange it for bread, perhaps,
in Łódź or – where was it he'd said?

V

Sojourner

What, at the end, was hard and worn and rounded
                              like the side of God,
like wood well turned, was home,
                              and must have been,
though, to my own mind, nothing but the old meandering
                              world and I lame.

I'd found all manner of thing in my father's barn –
                              harrow, rest-harrow –
though he was gone, like hired men after harvest festival,
                              the barn doors fallen,
the swifts not come.

Still there, the bowls and water-butts of rain, of sorrow,
                              gathered in.
Stored there, the spare sails for the windmill.

What was hard to understand –
                              the holes
in everything, the held wings
                              broken.

Child

She is heavier than air, a little heavier.

I shall carry her on my shoulder.

How did I come by her? Did I beget her?

Can I, how can I, abandon her to her stony desolation?

I shall walk with her as if I wore the whole Sahara on my shoulder –
wind, sand, sun and all of it frail as an aeroplane-
shadow and whole.

She has come to me.

'She is frail now, frail,' my mother said of her mother,
my grandmother in the cottage hospital.

'The light shows through her, she is full
of holes

and, when I lift her, lighter, almost,
than air.'

The New Broom
(for my mother)

Sarah, Alice she may have been –
servant to Julian of such long standing –

making her way among martyrs, cloth-merchants, men,
with her new broom.

Nothing will come to her now, a lost coin, a king.

Laughter – great leaps of it follow her home.

NOTE: Sarah and Alice were, at different times, servants
to Julian of Norwich in her 14th century anchorage.

Avice to Thomas in Mid-life
(for Clara)

What shall we do with the morning light that lies like new cloth?
Shall we measure it?
Shall we make wedding-gowns?

There are, I'd say, a dozen Aprils in it,
though it is May now and we need not plight our troth
again.

Earth is but earth,
its rough and ready stone,
and the light that lies upon our shoulders lightly worn.

NOTE: The Latin inscription on the Mildmay Monument in Chelmsford Cathedral, translated, reads:

'Here are seen the graven images of Thomas Mildmay and Avice his wife, but within their remains lie at peace. He was a renowned esquire, she a daughter and lovely branch of William Gunson Esq., and they had fifteen pledges of their prosperous love; seven whereof were females, eight were males.

Afterwards, in the year of Our Lord 1557, and in the morning of the 16th day of September, Avice returned to the dust from whence she originally sprang, and on the 10th day of the calends of October, in the ninth year following, the unrelenting king of terrors triumphed over Thomas.'

The Camellia House
(for Harriet Tarlo)

Mama made lace.

I did not think he would leave us.
I thought he could camp in the old camellia house.
Mama said so, loudly, at breakfast.

We liked the camellia house because of its glass,
its damp, flagged stone,
its cobwebs of wrought iron.

Camellias, she said, uncomprehending, old as bone.

A winter house, she said, in which a hundred years have gone.

Mama made lace.

I did not think he would leave us.

But he called for a kist of his own and a horse
and was gone.

Willem's Wife

Deaf as a church door, Magdalena, felt no fear.
He talked of her

as if she were the caught
quiet

of well or wood
in winter.
          Not a word she said

but sat before
the fire

alert
as a heart,

imaginative, mild –
          until the last child

lay athwart
her, like the thought

of fear
itself, the devil at the door.

Dolores' Afternoon

Mother's a bed on wheels.

We live among pomanders, within our own
　　espaliered walls.

We live in peril.

We don't love anyone at all.

Like larkspur, we are largely idle.

Or like silver somehow we've inherited.

Sometimes, in our stead, you'll see a spinning-wheel,
　　a wedding, a child born dead.

Dora, or Dido, buried beneath the yew where, later, we'll dawdle,
　　examining arils.

The Lady Balaton and I

Her face is bare, as if it were of wood.
Her lace is made.
Long ago now she married the lord, my uncle,
Who rowed her over the ornamental water.
Where is her loud Hungarian sister?
Now there are only herself, myself, and a man
To bring in logs.
One day her heart will break like a blackbird's egg.

Wiltshire, 1931

The Flower Rota: May Margaret in 1953

Her thoughts, she said, were an abandoned crow's nest –
Gethsemane with Christ gone and the gate left open banging in
                                            the wind
and all the king's horses and all the king's men.

She came to the altar with cut chrysanthemums,
fern from her garden, twine,
tidy as a Guild in her apron.

The ship with her son had gone down outside Rotterdam –
dredger or merchantman, it was all the same.
She'd hang on, she said, like the last of the apples, wasp-bitten.

Exile, Newcastle, 1962

My mother, thwarted.
A Grand Man by Catherine Cookson.
Gran getting old in London,
the lino in holes –
'You'll catch your heel!'
The Flight of the Heron by D.K. Broster (a woman).
My first period.

Convent Girl

They wearied me with prayer.

In the darkening garden of the dene, I stared.

I sought him where the way was unprepared, a wild rose.

The old road with its white line will not come again,

nor my heart with its old-fashioned indicators,

but my riven father

who knows.